# Martin Luther King Jr.
# and Other Poems

# Martin Luther King Jr. and **Other Poems**

*The Calm Strength of Humanity*

Yemi D. Ogunyemi

RESOURCE *Publications* • Eugene, Oregon

MARTIN LUTHER KING JR. AND OTHER POEMS
The Calm Strength of Humanity

Copyright © 2025 Yemi D. Ogunyemi. All rights reserved. Except for brief quotations in critical publications or reviews, no part of this book may be reproduced in any manner without prior written permission from the publisher. Write: Permissions, Wipf and Stock Publishers, 199 W. 8th Ave., Suite 3, Eugene, OR 97401.

Resource Publications
An Imprint of Wipf and Stock Publishers
199 W. 8th Ave., Suite 3
Eugene, OR 97401

www.wipfandstock.com

PAPERBACK ISBN: 979-8-3852-4062-3
HARDCOVER ISBN: 979-8-3852-4063-0
EBOOK ISBN: 979-8-3852-4064-7

VERSION NUMBER 04/24/25

## By the Same Author

**Novels**
The Melodrama of the Last Word
My Gazar With My Geisha
The Enchantress of Triple A
Modicums of O
Make Me Your Own
Twice Anagram
The Myths of the Coffee Boys
The Dreams of Joy
The Sweet Mother
The Talking River
The Last Cowrie Queen
The Literary Philosophy for the Year 2000
The Voice of the Earth
Ajayi Crowther's Piano

**Novelettes/Novellas**
My Sworn Friends
The Demise of a Would-be Title-Holder
Pursuit of Wisdom
(Sub-Title: A Divine Story that Never Ends)

**Short Stories**
The Chief Who Married 35 Wives
The Yellow House

Follow Me
Aduke is a Singer, Mama
Okobaba and the Nine Angels
Tortoise, the Storyteller
Waiting for the Dry Season
Vendetta
A Divine Story that Never Ends
My Beautiful Sister
Letters from Our Empire
The Floating Bungalow
How Leke Rescued Keke

**Poetry**
The Anthologies of the Diaspora
The Covenant of the Earth
The African Soul
The New Talking Drum
The Dawn of Tomorrow
M-A-S-T-A-M-A-N-D-A
Sued for Paternity
Codes of Morality
The Danger of a Single Rejection
Quid Pro Quo and Other Narratives
Path to Ifetheraphy and Its Healing Poems
The World, in a Fume of Pandemic Anxiety
How to Erase Racism from the Minds of Humanity
Lyric Boston—A City of Sisterly Love
Lagos—A City of Sisterly and Brotherly Love
The Undemocratic and Racist Amalgamation

Vienna, a City of Discreet Love and Women
Jumping Gaps of Prejudices and Racisms

## Children's Stories
The Source of River Koku
How Dogs Become Friends of Men
Why Mother Vulture Lost Her Neck Feathers
Tortoise, the Wisest Creature
January–December Lyrics
Why Giraffes Have Long Necks
A Hut Never Hurts
Why a Cock Cannot Crow
The Belling of the Wild Cat
Why Catty-Coo Chases Mousy-Loo
Jumbo and Piggy
Butti and Moti
How Zebras Got Their Whites and Black Stripes
My First Dream
How Tortoise Survived the Famine in Ogba
The Muddy Glade
Why Daddy Was Called Ho, Ho, Ho
How Lulu Became a Swimmer
The Missing Child
How Kemi and Layo Started Schooling
The Postman and His Son
Tortoise, My Friend
Why Grasshoppers Hop
Time for Competition
The House an Elephant Built
A Day with a Hunter

My Daddy's Sweet Potatoes
How Hoody and Hoofy Became Soccer Players
How the Lion Became the King of the Beasts
Why & How the Elephant Got His Huge Ears
The Ostrich and the Boomerang
Talk to me, I am Listening, O Angel
The Bee that Keeps her Promise
Why Jako Shoots without Missing
My Neighbor's Diary
Long Live the Queen
Mama, Let Me Be Me
The Song of a River
Why Bullying is Not Good
How the Hen Made the Cock a Happy Crower
How Maria and Bobby Became Friends
When the Children Are Difficult To Teach
Mom, It Is An Improper Overtaking
The Bald Valley Village
How Honey Came to the World
How Cowries Came to the World

**Actualities**
Yoruba Idealism
Literatures of the African Diaspora
Introduction to Yoruba Philosophy, Religion and Literature
Yoruba Philosophy and the Seeds of Enlightenment
The Birth of a Child in a Fishing Boat
The Aesthetic and Moral Art of Wole Soyinka
The Literary/Political Philosophy of Wole Soyinka
The Oral Traditions In Ile-Ife

Women in Europe
Media in Africa
The Political Ideas for Peace & Development in Nigeria
My Contact with Africans and Africa (Editor)
The Writers and Politics
The Birth of a Yoruba Nation
The Methodical Literary Criticism
Literary Criticism
(Subtitle: In Defense of the Humanities)

**Drama**
Three Plays
Obama, the Pragmatic President
(Subtitle: The Ankh of Progress)
King Oduduwa Comes to Americas and Europe

## Dedication–1

Dedicated to Paterfamilias Reuben O. Ogunyemi and Materfamilias Matilda A. Ogunyemi (nee Ikuemonisan) for putting me wise to heuristic education without a wrong construction.

## Dedication–2

Dedicated to Martin Luther King (1929-1968), for his calm strength of knowledge and for his vision for human dignity worldwide, without some pregnant constructions.

## Dedication–3

Dedicated to the champions of the 21st Century Enlightenment Movement, the Yoruba Philosophy and the Yoruba Idealism for embracing Myths and Weave, the Literary and Artistic Movement in the 9th Century Monarchical Yoruba Country.

## Dedication–4

Dedicated to Divinity-Philosopher Ogun, the connoisseur and commander-in-chief of arts who lets me know that the work of art, poetry especially, is like magic. Sometimes it astonishes. Sometimes it mystifies. Sometimes it seizes one and carries one captive. Sometimes it is like a scherzando. Sometimes it strengthens the imagination by sharpening its delicacy and enlarging its ranges, purviews and nuances. The work of art is beautiful, a marvel of ingenuity.

**Contents**

*My Sub Rosa and Personal Dedication To Ijapa* | xiii
*Introduction: What My Parents Told Me* | xv
*Author's Lodestar and Abridged Memoir* | xix
*In Defense of Description* | xxiii

Part One: **In the Beginning, There Was/Is a Word** | 1

Part Two: **The Stars of the Star-lets** | 27

Part Three: **The Star of Enlightenment (That Illuminates Within Us)** | 63

Part Four: **Chief Awo's Exceeding Joy, 1959** | 73

Part Five: **My Goal In Life (My Crown of Jewels)** | 79

Part Six: **The Nine Cardinal Virtues of the Yoruba Folk Philosophy** | 107

Part Seven | 117

Part Eight | 121

Epilogue: **Fait Accompli** | 133

*Author Bio:* | 135

## My Sub Rosa and Personal Dedication To Ijapa

Dedicated to the nonpareil storyteller whose mononymous name is Ijapa: he will always be remembered as my great teacher. He put me through Yoruba fairytales and folklore, and stories with ends and stories without ends. He lets me know that every letter of the Yoruba alphabet (from A-Y), has a story attached to it. This makes me think mononymous Ijapa has a predilection to magic like the fairies, the small/diminutive beings with magic powers.

    My intellectual and artistic virtuosity is not complete without appreciating Ijapa as the greatest fabulist that ever lived in Yoruba country. Mononymous Ijapa whose poetic name is Protatoise is the folk hero and the fabled protagonist of antiquity of the Yoruba folktales. He is noted for his legal fiction, his polite fiction, his folk etymology and his folk memory. Additionally, his epistemology of the Yoruba culture is far-reaching, making one feel that he knows many things much as he cultivates many things pertaining to the Yoruba cultural values. Although he was a grandiloquent paradox of a teller, he was nonetheless a thinking thinker who essays to avoid and deracinate many farragoes of nonsense or useless knowledge (smattering) that had marred his reputation, for so long, as an inimitable teller imbued with blue blood or a teller from the royal house. Acting like a sponger in the house of hospitality and living in genteel poverty was un-regal and ridiculous, demonstrative of his bag-eyed behavior. Because of this singular behavior, his critics regard him as a cockalorum adept in cunnings and dissimulations whose prosopographies make him a queer specimen of humanity.

## Introduction
What My Parents Told Me

During my formative years, between the age of 5 and 13, when I was enjoying the benefits of juvenilia—carving, weaving and drawing, my parents (adept in classic fairy-tales) told me that King Oduduwa was the first patriotic scion of the Yoruba country. They let me know that he is/was a noble man with nobiliary particles, born in the celestial Throne of Grace and re-born in the awe-inspiring settlement of Ile-Ife which is today known as the holy city of Ile-Ife, a city of over 500,000 stakhanovite inhabitants, in the present-day Yoruba land (country), flowing with organic milk and honey. King Oduduwa was a humble and gentleman, made to the character of a devout, happy in everything but putting no more faith in anything than the Book of Enlightenment—the Ifa-Ife Divination. According to them, not without some pregnant constructions, his dynasty was crème de la crème, peaceful, artistic and very resourceful throughout his reign of many decades with the benefit of the holy gourd, *the holy gourd of longevity, wellness and happiness.*

"Treat everyone with love and respect. We are the same from the same Family Tree, from the same umbilical cord of muliebrity/motherhood, from the taproot of the Family Tree to its apex. Therefore, regard everyone as your brother, sister, prince or princess. We are the same one blue blood from Oduduwa dynasty," they asserted with perfect aplomb.

My parents did not only put me wise to it, they succeeded in putting me up to it by adjuring me to break ranks with any pedantry (chop logic) and my solipsistic narrow-mindedness. They added that I should have an algorithmic knowledge of all the major divinities who are theophorically connected to Creator-Philosopher Olodumare. These theophoric divinities are Oduduwa, Obatala, O'Sango, Ogun, Orunmila, O'Yemoja, Osun, O'Sopona, Oya, O'Esu, Olokun and Ososi. They enjoined me to believe in arts, adding that art, a marvel of ingenuity, a symbol of reality, is an expression of happiness, an application of human creative skill. They constantly remind me that Creator-Philosopher Olodumare is an inimitable designer-artist who designed all the creatures. Knowing that there is an artist in every household in Yoruba land, and believing that art is made for life's sake and not for art's sake, I said to my parents that it suits my book to become an artist and belong to the league or class of intellectuals and artistic virtuosity. Cornucopian smiles of innocent conscience flirted with my five senses, impelling me to compare myself to a cognate object, because a cognate object is an object that is related in origin and sense to the verb governing it, as in *live a good life*.

As I grew up year by year, I understand that I, like other artists have to work within Nature's purview. Also, it becomes opalescent clear to me that of all aesthetic things/arts on the surface of the earth and under the vault of heaven, none is as aesthetic as the art-rainbow.

The Revelation of the Nonpareil Storyteller: My parents adjured me to respect the nonpareil teller whose mononymous name is Ijapa and to always pay homage to him. According to them, mononymous Ijapa is versed in myth and weave. It was the literary and artistic movement in Yoruba country in circa 9th century when every myth and weave was thought to be the divine will of Olorun/Olodumare (amuwa Olorun/Olodumare). It was the period of oral literature when mononym was the order of the day. (It was a pre-soft-pedaling revolution but

Ijapa lets us know that it was a pre-artistic revolution in Yoruba country).

How Did It Start? It started when the heads of the people (full of mints of ideas filtering through people's minds) were merry with myths and artistic works, when there was an artist in every household, when the literary arts could not be taken for triviality; the society began to find happiness and the meaning of life in their mythological tales and artworks. This happiness and meaningful life led to the soft-pedaling movement which is known as myth and weave. It has since then become a tradition segueing from those oral recording and experience to the present age of pen and paper.

With stress and rhythm, cognate with the admission that learning is a cumulative process, it was a novel dawn in the life of a nation, and what's more, the 9th century symbolizes the age when aesthetics is regarded the appreciation of philosophy of nature, beauty and arts.

They emphasized that mononymous Ijapa was the greatest storyteller Yoruba country has ever produced. By the time he paid his debt to Nature (many keepers of traditions inferred that he did not die but disappeared like fairies) in the twelfth century, he was credited with thousands of tales/stories.

This is what mononymous Ijapa said of himself, "With respect to my lung power, and while taking care of number one, I am the folk hero and the fabled protagonist of antiquity of Yoruba folktales. I am no skeleton dragged out of the shadows to dance a bone dance in the middle of the leading strings. Those who know my long history will vouchsafe for me that I am a downright folk philosopher who works like a Stakhanovite since the days of pre-dynasty."

*The following is his prose experience with the crown of jewels: The crown of jewels whose opalescent jewels shine in the shine of the moon, whose first gleams of the morning sun glitter upon the earth, has a metaphorical history of crowning many heads of our Oyo Emperors. It had extolled the practice of love in Yoruba country. It had served as the emblem of unity and solidified the kingdom of the holy city of Ile-Ife and reinforced the Staff of Creation. This crown of opalescent jewels, thou art the crown that gives birth to other crowns.*

I was so delighted and grateful to my kind-loving parents. Because I was delighted and grateful, I was tempted to turn a verb into a verbal noun, otherwise known and called a gerund. My fund of humor came to a happy remembrance with a warm and delicious dish of taramasalata and bouillabaisse.

## Author's Lodestar and Abridged Memoir
(The Calm Strength of Literary Philosophy)

If I should occupy myself by remembering the land of great antiquities, if I should recount all the artistic and the literary pleasures derived from my years of innocence, cognate with tableaux, if I should reflect upon the pleasures of memory and imagination from the years of childhood, I would feel full of vim due to my adrenaline glands. Grateful I am. I will feel sublime from inside to the outside and from outside to the inside, as though the descendants of the slavers had settled the reparations for purloining our ancestors from the continent of blue blood. My appetite for literature (my propaedeutic genre) will continue to increase, as I grow from year to year, while my appetite for comestible will be controlled or circumscribed by the pleasures obtained from the reams of writings. For good literature, which is the foundation of pleasures (like music rather than the media) nourishes the human emotions, reaffirms the present and reconstructs the future. These ethical and rational beliefs and assertions are inexhaustibly fundamental and interesting by the contents of their canons of conduct.

Relating all this with mankind and seeking the pleasures of relationships are the greatest sources of happiness that one can derive from the calm strength of humanity, regaling upon the virtue of philosophy, literature and arts, yes–true to the province of aesthetics.

The calm strength of love, found in humanity and the feeling of writing, dovetailing with the artistic virtuosity is like the feeling derived from listening to the delicious music of the spheres. An intellectual had asked, "Why do you write?" I write because my writing could become one of the soft-pedaling means to promote/enhance peace and love around the world. I write because the mortals and immortals expect me to write. I write because I want to be read, and read others. I write because I have fallen head over heels in love with letters, books and the power of words. I write because Creator-Philosopher Olodumare is my teacher and my director and my giver who always gives me mints of ideas that filter through my mind. I write because I invariably find an organic happiness in writing. I write because writing qualifies me to belong to the class/league of sciences and the humanities. I write because writing therapeutically distils my mind. I write because I want my writing to belong to the archives and libraries of immortality. I write because writing helps me link my existence to saints, angels, geniuses and heroes. I write because I want the Oversoul to explain to me why there are so many mysteries and tragicomedies in the world. I write because I want my writing to refresh the memories of the loved ones whose departures make my heart trapped in melancholy. I write in order to know myself and what myself can do to help everyone, my neighbor, since everyone is my friend with the charity of love. I write because I want my writing to inform, enlighten, entertain, educate, inspire, charm/enchant, and above all, inoculate the world with the ingredients of wellness, corporeal and spiritual happiness, likened to the thrills of a sweet dream.

    On noticing that I am still one-third a writer I would love to be, my parents who always stand on ceremony, in their hours of happiness, nobility, pleasantries and gleam of humor, demand of me the loftiest, the best, the crème de la crème, the noblest and the most supreme that I can do, but much that I could by no possibility have done, in order to belong to the league/class of sciences and the humanities, and be guided by the literary philosophy, and the power of words, as reason guides the human soul to nirvana or sasarawa.

Yemi D. Ogunyemi, Prof. (also known as Yemi D. Prince) (Literary Philosopher)

## In Defense of Description

The writing of Martin Luther King and Other Poems gestated in 2018 shortly after the successful completion and publication of Yoruba Philosophy and the Seeds of Enlightenment. The work is divided into Eight Parts. While Part One is the masthead—the poetic biography of Martin Luther King, Part Two through Part Eight is a crown of jewels worn by many heads, poetizing and epigrammatizing in the calm strength of knowledge and humanity, cognate with constructive metabolism.

# PART ONE

## In the Beginning, There Was/Is a Word

## Prologue

In a devout family, born in 1929
Heralding the American Depression
At a time when racial segregation
Was like the Jinn and terrorist let out
From demijohn/St George Terror Gin's Bottle

A ruling passion copulated with his
Cognomen, crown-fitted head
African kingdom, the burden of proof
In his maiden dream, God had said
He would raise him to raise the world

Ere racial slurs tear apart the land
Loved to commune with God every day
From his heart of hearts,
He vowed to make a difference, a change
With the help of Creator-Philosopher Olodumare

*Remember, I'll be with you in every step you take*
*And in every corner you negotiate*
*You've been equipped with the voice needed to deliver*
*Your forthcoming nationwide dream/prophetic message*
*My Holy Spirit is sufficient for you, therefore, Ase.*

## Who Shall I Send? 1954!

A triangle, formed like a miracle, on a panhandle
Jutting out equilaterally, to the Atlantic
Inside this triangle, there were 300 able-bodied
Men and women in motley dresses
One hundred lined soldierly each one
Of the three edges of the triangle

Suddenly, there was a voice—**who shall I send?**
A basso profondo voice rejoined—here I am send me
*A task there is: a task that must be done*
*Can you accomplish this task for mankind?*
Yes, I will with might and main
Aided by my adrenaline glands
*Even if you sacrifice your life for it?*

Yes, O Lord: my God
Your task is more precious than my life
*Are you ready to uplift the world?*
*From a ridiculous situation to a sublimity*
With faith and with your spiritual vim
I will, just like the Son of Man.

## The Historical Inception, 1955

Many prayers offered day and night
Before and after his doctorate
Mobilizing his spiritual energy to uplift his
Kith and kin from political and economic doldrums
To the standard required by milk of human kindness
Yearning for universal love, freedom and equality

Heads of Thought Men and Women put together
The beginning of the whys and the bathos
Aurora-borealis, the unmistakable sign
From Creator-Philosopher God
The prophetic voice has been uttered
Martin Luther King had imbibed the voice

Saying, from the breast of the earth
I have been nursed to know my history
A free slave: no more an exile
But a patriotic citizen in his second home
God I will humbly thank for making me
Reject all that's rejectable

The voice of man in love with the voice of God
Gave birth to the **Civil Rights Movement**
After the sign in the firmament
Martin Luther King knew then

A battle of words and protests
Are inevitable, for
Enough is enough

ASEPO-DARA=UNITY IS GOOD
If only we can come together
We will be able to fight this justifiable battle
A corporeal and spiritual battle
Needed to protect us
And our children in this land
The land that belongs to one and all
God-given land, in adoration of humanity.

**Charmingly Entranced**
In a high brow meeting of
Thought Men and Women
Not divined for my kindred
Surprisingly entranced with decorum
Even if my seat invisible in the rear
Defined by a penumbra and a halo
As I sat down, feathering my nest
Here, a man, hiding a beatific smile
He saw me ere my eyes
Upon him clapped.

"I have a dream for you,"
He enunciated in a basso profondo
"What are the contents of your dream?"
"In my dream, I beheld a letter **A**
Etched upon your marble forehead

I will be gone when you are there
Be fearless, thou shall be fearless
Thou shall be brave like a lion
Life is an admixture of smooth and rough."

Before the meeting folded up
I asked, where are you going to?
I am going to join the long
Line of our pedigrees
I must go now. Go I must
And continue to supplicate
For the loved ones left behind
The struggle continues
May you enjoy **A**, the land of dreams!

No sooner I woke up than
I realized I had been in a calm strength
Of a prophetic dream
A fry, a mere termite . . .
I was absorbed in a nudging contemplation
Reflecting upon a civil voice
That would bring me to **A**
The land of dreams and dreamers.

A benevolent man, he was
Made to the character of the 20th century
Suspicious of the 1960s oppressors
Putting no more trust in the oppressors
Than our loving Creator-Philosopher God
If there is any prophecy

Worth noticing and analyzing in the 20th century
His prophecy will take the front seat
On the tongues of our ancestors/pedigrees.

The demonstrators shall be mobilized
Across the four corners of the land
We shall march and sing in unity
We shall fast and pray in unity
Our voices shall be heard around the world
Our guide and guardian is solely the Holy Spirit
There shall be no unthinking moment
That may be compared to Oshosi-cum-Ogun-like Capoeira
Or the Mau Mau, not even Umkhonto we Sizwe
This is a Civil Rights Movement
Things that are equal to the same
Are equal to one another!
We simply want the government to vouch
For equal rights and to honor human rights
Peacefully, nonviolently, equal in treatment.

## Your Bravery Thunders Me
## Martin Luther King

Martin Luther King, your bravery thunders me
Your heroism, recognized posthumously
Your Birthday, etched on a marble stone
But we will talk about your valor
That shakes heaven and earth
Like the roars of thunders in the rainy season.

**The Ruse from 1954:** *Stay put under oppression*
*Better to be oppressed than leave*
*For your original continent of blue blood*
*And face starvation*
*See pictures of malnutrition and lack of infrastructure*
*Call it a vehicle of manipulation.*

Martin Luther King, your bravery frightens me
Will you let their keep-them-down tactics?
Take advantage of your pastoral love
Sabotaging your equality drive
Do you bear a razor blade, a knife,
An assegai, a catapult, a bazooka.
A machete, a tomahawk, a shotgun,
A natural bullet-proof vest?
None of the above for self-defense?

What do you have to shield yourself?
From a fatal assault, except the Holy Books
Oh Martin Luther King
Your kingdom of Thought baffles me.

Our women are tearful but not weeping
Our men are concerned but not giving up
Our children are impatient but not un-adorable
By not remembering the milk of human kindness
Is to be called no longer noble
Our backs are pushed to the walls
Let's settle our supremacist differences
And wipe out our overflowing tears
With a dirty white handkerchief

## The Crusade Against Inequality

What a day of blissfulness
When the palomino
Will gallop to the sky and open
The sky's cranny for the sun to shine
To beam over the earth
With a rapturous hymn of love

What a night of exultation
When the colorless steed
Will journey to the sky
To tap open the sky's door
For the moon and stars to sing
The long-awaited song of exultation

In your dream thou knoweth that something
Will happen to none but you
But to yourself, thou hast kept the dream
In bravery, man dies but once
No choice for a coward, but to die many times
Your bravery has empowered me, MLK

The atmosphere charged
But controlled by the holy hand
Your basso profondo voice shall mobilize

Every ear that listens to it
You voice, your voice designed to put balm
On every anxious soul

The ungodly human rights violations
A glaring eyesore, unbearable
Something must be done
Under one Creator-Philosopher God
We both love and worship daily
In unity, the world joined you in **1963's March
On Washington**, the nation's capital
As you vehemently and rhetorically said
Destroy all the structures of inequality
Destroyed; then the password to Happiness
We will pursue in peace and with passion

We are: we are marching to Washington
With discipline in our heads and respectful tongues
Minimizing trepidation. Maximizing valor
A cause so dear, so defined
We are marching on to Washington
Putting a voice to our Movement

The world would be listening
To the desires of young and old children
Of a humble beginning
Will be spelt out in twenty-six
English alphabet letters
Giving our ancestors a reason to rejoice

Standing upon a soapbox betwixt two rises
He kowtowed and prayed, "*God, you've sent me*
*Let the voice of the mighty*
*And the voice of the humble*
*The voice of the visible*
*And the voice of the invisible*
*Unite today to make this gathering a success*
*In the name of the Son of Man. Ase/Amen"*

Brushing your semicircle moustache, from left to right
Your basso profondo voice of prophecy boomed out
**I HAVE A DREAM**, a dream to the Promised Land
Edifying. Eloquently delivered the very year we lost
One of our activists and a sympathizer
Both thinking thinkers of love—JFK and Malcolm X
Supernovas against the moribund
Racism, too superannuated
To exist in the 20th century
Their demise, not a warning to you?

But you are not alone, in your quest to end racism
And racial slurs. Apart from your second half
And thousands of others, young and old
Motivated by Rosa Parks,
Of the legendary **Bus Boycott, 1955**
The first lady of the Civil Rights Movement
Do we still remember, how she dared to sit down
Yes, she sat down regally
Talked with a civil tongue, regally

Carried herself regally like Queen Moremi
Of the holy city of Ile-Ife

Civil Rights Movement, in its gamut of activities
A Birth of Re-awakening, philosophically
A Humanistic Movement in its own right
The legend of the God-send far richer
Than any poet-artist could imagine/invent

From the womb of our native land
To the womb of the slave ship
To the womb of our destination
Many have perished, needlessly
The psychological tears caused by disorientation
The nostalgic pains of separation
The see-saws of so many problems, encountered
The hell of excruciating tribulations
Would you let my people go in freedom?
Borrowing Luthuli's pleading words of sensibility

Hear our happy mean, this wall
Of racial segregation, disenfranchisement
Mean discrimination must be dismantled
A welcome joy receiving the **Nobel Peace Prize in 1964**
Was that the beginning of good things to happen?
Martin and his colleagues, followers wondered
The movement must continue, howbeit

Where is our peaceful and humble upbringing?
Threatened, threatened without anyone listening?

We've gone through many, how many shall we count?
The throes of life
The *wahalarobia* of life
The vicissitudes of life
The whirligigs of life
The insanity of life caused by slavery
The rains and reins of racial prejudices
The molestations of the young and old
The harassments of the vulnerable
Lynching not uncommon
Hanging not unusual
Imprisonments prevalent as mad-cow disease
Raping widespread as the breath of Mulattoes
Hatred inhaled and exhaled
Like the masters' cigar-smokes
To whom shall we point our index fingers?
Perpetrators, cultivators of these bag-eyed behaviors?

**Practical Jokes Unabated**
Practical jokes numerous, everyday
Back and forth the two continents
Most abused animals: guenon and canine
But they rebelled with the publication of
**Animal Farm, George Orwell, 1945**
They sacked their oppressors
And refused to be called scapegoats,
Putting kibosh on practical jokes
The race to sublime civilization betwixt them
And their oppressors, they won, outstandingly
Vociferating that as long as there is no

Racism in the Animal Kingdom
The erected walls of racism in Human Kingdom
Are uncivilized as they are un-Godly
Must be torn down like the Berlin walls

The movement must continue with vigor of purpose
Despite being awarded the **Nobel Peace Prize, 1964**
It shall move from a Civil Rights Movement
To a Civil Rights Revolution
The ears of our brothers and sisters
In Africa, Asia, Latin America and Europe
Are hearing the tintinnabulations of our cries
For justice and equal rights and mutual respects
Betwixt the coined supremacists and the blue blood

Why keeping us down?
The revolutionaries continue to demand
We are the same children of our Loving God
If you want to help the underdogs
Don't keep down the underdogs
While helping the underdogs
All we need is the opportunities to help ourselves
Let's embrace the civilization of equality, can we?

Our revolution/movement is non-violent,
Will never be violent
But its thunderous sound
Clarion loud amongst the willows
They are the ripples upon the waters
They are the ripples upon the grasses

They are the ripples amongst the clouds
Under the vault of heaven.

Hear our voices for freedom, oh God
You supplicated day and night

We salute our African ancestors/pedigrees
We greet those freedom fighters on the African continent
Now that the yokes of colonization are breaking down
That of Apartheid South Africa shall also break down
In spite of baiting Chief Albert John Luthuli
With Nobel Prize for Peace, 1961
The African freedom fighters
Will not fall into despondency
We will not slip into despondency
Hear me, our ancestors did not sell our
Kith and kin into slavery
Save a few: collaboration, yes they did
Due to your cunnings and dissimulations

Even if we've lost our teeth in your service
We know we did truly serve you
Fought your wars, truly, gallantly
Sporting medals, we received here and there
Why are you then angry with us?
Are we the moths that damaged?
The flowers, thus depriving the bees
From obtaining their nectars?
Can we gulp a little bit, a little bit of our
Labor from a land flowing with milk and honey?

Humanity, humanity, are we humans?
Why must we stoop low, so low to the ebb?
Comparing ourselves with guenon and canine?

Good news! We're rising from the bottom to the top
We will look down from lofty mountain grandeur
And juxtapose **I have a Dream**
With a Change is Gonna Come, Sam Cooke, 1964

This, a terra firma-like boat
Let's enter it with a cry for un-jaded love
Without anyone of us rocking it
Destined to be free from injustice
As divined and longed for by our ancestors
From the continent of the blue blood
The contents of our character likened to
The nine virtues contained in Yoruba codes of morality
Love, morality, temperance, honor, honesty, prudence
Justice, bravery and fortitude

Anything short of these codes of morality
Will be regarded a travesty of decorum
Needed to enjoy equal rights, our inalienable rights
Let's dismantle these walls, once and for all
Made of human skin colors
Then we'll climb the mount yonder to the top
To the Promised Land
I may not get there with you
But we will one day get there together
For in my dream, the dream I cherish

One day Black and White will appreciate each other
With the benefits of dignity, respect and love
Then the contents of man's character
Will no longer be judged by the skin color
But by the *iwalewa*, the quality of man's character
Then the world will leap for joy
Shimmying, jouncing, singing, ululating hosannas
Then a thunderous happy voice
We are free, we are free: free at last
Racial segregation tumbled into the Atlantic
Jim Crowism cremated and interred
Mean discrimination pulverized
The bullying under disfranchisement
Has vanished into oblivion

**Obsequial Eulogies after the fatality of
Martin Luther King, April 14, 1968**
All of a sudden, all eyes were closed
Ushering in a solemn silence
By the time the eyes were open
A gunshot heard, and gunpowder smelt
A few days later, a mournful cortege
To Morehouse College, yielding to his mournful burial
At MLK Center, Atlanta, after a National Day
Of Mourning that seemed not to end
People glued their eyes to the firmament
Watching Martin Luther King transform
Under the aura of Holy Spirit and immortality
Beneath the wisps of clouds
**I have a dream** echoed and re-echoed again

A hair-tiny mournful voice whispered, "Another Messiah
Has come and gone, unrecognized. How long will
They expect the Messiah to be born with a
Silver spoon in his mouth before they accept him
As their Lord and Savior?"

Akin to homilies, a king-like voice cooed,
*"Oh Creator-Philosopher God, if you've known me*
*And likened me to King Solomon, or Joseph*
*The Dreamer: if you've made me like those sons*
*In whom you're pleased, you could have*
*Empowered me to dream to avoid this*
*Fatal calamity which has befallen me*
*If you've known, as I know you know, you*
*Could not have allowed me to perish in*
*The hands of a shooter and bully of humanity*
*Who has no respect for any one upon this earth*
*Dying while my children so young and in need of*
*Their father, is the least dream man can dream*
*Since the outset of this all-purpose Movement*
*Indeed you could have caused the hater/shooter*
*To miss his target and hit his own shadow*
*But thy will be respected: thy will be done!"*

The lion of Civil Rights Movement has been
Forced to join the long line of our pedigrees
Too young to go to the realm of immortality
Too young to leave us behind, unprotected
While the struggle continues
Too young to be cut short

At the cusp of his exuberance
Black-brown-proud faces
Turned lugubrious with tears
Cascading upon their shoulders as though
They were under the eaves during the tropical
Rainy season in Atlantic Yoruba land.

An illustrious son has been assassinated!
The entire world, shocked, crestfallen
Nevertheless ideas to survive continue, one of which
The philosophical and historical creation
The first Black Studies Department in 1968
Heralding other ethnic studies departments
Kwanzaa came into being, 1967
Black-Brown of "I am black and proud"
Christened African-Americans, 1988
Oyotunji African Kingdom established, 1970
Black History Week, originated by Carter Woodson 1961
Developed into **Black History Month** since 1970
Embracing historical events of Africans in Diaspora
Then another aurora-borealis
Flirting above the cloud scrapers
Then the audacity of hope and dreams, born
Giving birth to the hugest political, economic and social
Metamorphosis in the 21st century: dreams of love
As **Barack Obama** rose to take reins of
The highest office in the country, President 2009-20017

In the 1960s, the roaring 1960s
Many falls and rises, there were
Surprisingly, there continued to sprout
The facelift of tolerance, rationality
Dialogue, accommodation and common sense

Martin Luther King, thou hast opened the door
To the land of dreams and dreamers
People from the West
People from the East
People from the North
People from the South
Started milling to **A** in droves
Martin Luther King Junior
You've shed your dear blood
For a humane **A**, the land of dreams
Words of gratitude: MLK, we love you
For sacrificing your dear life
For one and all—children of the Providence
Now joining delightfully the League
Of our divine and reverential ancestors
We appreciate you and your colleagues
As we celebrate your 90th Birthday today,
**January 21**, 2019, a centenarian,
Ten years short: but your **National Holiday**
Strongly advocated by Stevie Wonder
Ethically and lawfully granted in **1986**
**Continues as one of your dignified**
**Mnemonic and moral legacies.**

We rejoice, gladly too
Even if some gang-areas are peaceful
But not without weapons of self-defense

The calabooses are crowded
But not tearing down

Liquor stores holding discussion groups
But not without psychotropic drinks

The Worshipping Houses are not scared
But not without the Holy Spirit guarding them

I will tell you what God
Has revealed to me
Do tell me if I am off the mark.

Man is re-created by what he loves
And haunted by what he hates.

Watching us, and jealously too
Are the Black Panther, "panthering us day and night
Garbed in nondescript camouflage
Vigilantly, sentineling, standing guard
Under the commander-in-Chief of Oshosi
Striking the much-needed balance
Betwixt the rough-pedaling lovers
And the smooth-pedaling lovers

## From 1954 to 2019: From 20th to 21st Century

Today, Now: inducted into the Hall of Fame
You will look back from the blessed Hall of Fame
Of our Ancestors, the beloved
Hall of Fame and Dignity
And behold the catalogue of struggles
A near-revolution struggle
Black Struggle Movement
Black Power Movement
Black Lives Matter, fresh on the historians' tongues
Soft-pedaling believers in equality,
Increased from 45 percent to 95 percent
Oh Creator-Philosopher God/Olodumare
Let the ashes and vestiges of bullying
Be cast into the bottom of the blue
Now that **A** had risen from the ashes of paganism
Your MLK statuettes symbolizing your sacrifice
Love, struggle for equality and end of racism
You will be happy to cachinnate with gusto
For things are metamorphosing for the better
Men and women have graduated with laurels
From the Kingdom of Thought in the 20th century
To the kingdom of Reasoning in the 21st century.

**A New Dawn**
    **Done**
      **Down**
        **Up**
          **Dawn**
            **Up**

Up to the Promised Land
MLK, your ideal dream
More than half-realized
It's enough to be thankful to you
It's enough to be grateful to you

Up, upon the mountain grandeur
We'll pour our ablutionary libation by the tarn
With the soft-pedaling believers
And the hard-pedaling believers
We'll sing the same uplifting hymn

As contained in the world Holy Books
We shall bow down our heads
In solemn supplications
And solemnize loud and clear
"We appreciate you, Martin Luther King."

After reading: The Origin of Others
No longer a conundrum, visible
No longer invisible, on coming out of the cage
Rejoicing and Appreciating that
Race no longer matters

After reading The Souls of Black Folk, 1903
And offer Prayers for Dark People
And Against Racism
And analyze the circumstances leading to
"I can't breathe. I can't breathe. I can't breathe."

After we must have toasted
To our health from the gourd of palm-wine
That renewed itself on its own accord
And then devoured my favorite
Dish of taramasalata and roe. Ase.

# PART TWO

## The Stars of the Star-lets

## Born to See the Sanity of Life

I was born to see a river
And everything by the river
Alive and full of sanity of life
The beauty of life cannot be compromised
I have many dreams, some serene
Some rough, intimidating and formidable
But I will never give up
Following the path of sanity even if
Ceilings falling
Stars falling
Mountains stumbling
And I ask myself:
What is happening to the sanity of the world?
The meek and the weak crying for justice
Why must the small fingers suffer in perpetuity?
Why must man stoop low
Like the donkeys, like the goats, like the sheep
Stolen by the big fingers from our compound
How can the small fingers overcome?
The brutality of the big and callous fingers
When shall the innocent
Sing their own song of freedom and justice?

## Sanity of Life

Creative juices derived from the river
Creative inspiration by the river, derived
Creative voice heard by the river
Creative passion by the river, my felicity
Creative songs lured me
Into the river, swimming
Swimming, trying to cross the river
Overhead, the bulbuls
Lilting a healing song
Designed to heal the river-water
Of its constant pollution.

## Before Our Very Eyes

Lo and behold! See the eyes that see
See more than they see
See the ears that hear
Hear more than they hear
The mouths that eat
Eat more than they eat.

Dimmed with tears, my eyes
Seeing, witnessing
All the fishes of every description
Dying out of existence,
Upshot of the pollution
Sorrily, I felt helpless, indecisive
What else remains but to scoop the dead fishes?
Out of the river
The river by whose bank I was born
And supplicating, ceaselessly, happily
In the hope of seeing the continuity
      Of
The sanity of life.

## The Voices of Our Children

Delight in me
My delight in you
Thou art my forget-me-not
A voice, loud and clear
Came from our children.

The voices of our children
And the voice of the cared
The voice of the present
And the voice of the future
The voice of all that would say
Laud those who are caring
For the earth, if sane
Its sanity would save
And sanitize one and all.

## A Poem from a River Maid

**If** you listen to me
**Wherever** you're
**There's** always from me
**A** story of Happiness
**Driving** away sadness.

**I** greet the world
**In** dancing and singing
**Sharing** my smiles with waves
**And** ripples of felicity.

**My** passion has always cured the sick
**Quenching** the thirsty throats
**Washed** away the body clad with dirt
**I** have thrilled the heroes and heroines
**Who** came to me telling their stories
**Of** woes and perilous adventures.

## A 19th Century Rescued Slave Talking to His Mother

Mother, mother, if you had known
As I know, you did not know
When you last saw me.

Like other mothers
You did not know
I know you did not know.

For if you had known
You could not have asked me
To become a basket weaver.

The occupation that got me
Into this trouble of being enslaved
This inhuman business of slavery.

Which I know
As you know
I am happy, sure to say I hate.

## The Spirit of the American Dreams

In the midst of the Holy Spirit
Gliding and wafting
Like the eagles under the cerulean skies
Like the homing pigeons
Perching and taking off
Under an azure of a day.

I found my eyes
Glued to the Holy Spirit
Inhaling and exhaling majestically
Relishing the calm strength of the Holy Spirit
Like an aura enjoying the fullness of life.

Suddenly, I found myself
Inside a spirit-borne balloon
A Holy Spirit by name
Supplicating and dreaming
Smiling and frolicking.

As the spirit-borne balloon
Landed betwixt a seaport and an airport
As the hordes of welcomers
Welcoming me and saying,
"Welcome, thou dreamer, to the land of dreams."

**Underwater Lyrics**

Even if it's a short one
I will say this with undiluted confidence
I will lyricize underwater
And rise above the rippling crests
Like a happy, playful dolphin
And pronounce with certainty and confidence
The most heartfelt and positive world on earth
Which is **L-O-V-E**
That files you and I together: Believe me!
HAPPY MOTHER'S DAY! **L-O-V-E!**

**Easter**

For the believers
For the soft-and-fast-pedaling believers
Easter, a period of joy
Wrapped with
Happiness that
Never ends with
The resurrection of
Jesus Christ.

## The Law of Stability betwixt him and her

For all that has been and would be
A little bit of understanding
A little bit of unconditional love
A little bit of peace
A little bit of prayer-faith
A little bit of tolerance
A little bit of caress
A little bit of whisper
A little bit of determination
A little bit of smiles and laughter
A little bit of selflessness
A little bit of ethical/moral behavior
Will make the world
The Paradise: the Promised.

## A Memento at Forty

At my fortieth birthday
Presented, a shining mask of Obalufon
Made of terracotta
My gratitude infinite
Like the Love of Creator-Philosopher Olodumare
He told me to preserve the ageless artwork
Told him it is not enough to preserve
What we already have, we must also find
Means to create things we do not have

Why must it be ageless, I asked him
Because the foreign archaeologists
Say it is about 12th century. Maybe much earlier
But our native archaeologists can say otherwise
If they don't obsequiously believe in speculative philosophy
They had better find out the truth
In lieu of speculative philosophy
Let Creative-Philosopher Olodumare guide them
As reason guides the human soul.

**The Final Say**

Who has the final say?
Asked the congregation
My rejoinder, Olodumare
Has the final say
The Unknown challenging the Known
The Known challenging the Unknown
Who has the final say?
But Creator-Philosopher Olodumare!

## The Beginning

The beginning (the past) is 1
The present added to the beginning =1+6=7
When the past is subtracted from the present=7-1=6
I have imbibed more ideas in my present
Than in the past, in the beginning
I have perched upon the shoulders of the past
In order to delight in the present
One will always remain 1
Even if the world stumbles into the deep
Upside down, spreading its insoluble fragments
People scurrying helter-skelter
Searching for drops of water to quench their thirst
I may be forced to change my theory
But nothing will change my belief
In addition and subtraction
Even if my alter ego
Is forced to sip from
A calabash bowl of boiling fat

## Hurrah! We Are Enfranchised

We gave libations to our pedigrees
We cachinnated so much, Sango-like
Until aches were registered on our sides
And our palpable thankful prayers,
"We thank you Creator-Philosopher Olodumare
Let the kingdom of reason always defeat
The kingdom of un-reason."

## The Artworks in Open-Air Museums

All found in open-air museums
All these artworks basking in the sun
They may be without their makers
Their archaeological history
May have been lost in antiquity
What remains but
But a speculative philosophy
That baffles one and all

Weather-wise, nature in love
Blooms in harmony
With serene imagination
Ideal for these antiquaries
Their eyes glowing with smiles of happiness
Carrying bags, ones and twos
Ready for their competition-like haggling.

## The Teachings of My Father

Pa taught me many, many a thing
He taught me to reach the
Highest shelf, standing upon his stool
He taught me to reach for the paradise
And the immortality seeds
At the bottom of the long-necked gourd
In all his teachings
He demanded of me
Not to reach only the utmost
That I could reach
But much I could by no
Possibility could have reached

**My Sustainer–1**

What the Heart has left undone
What the Mind has left undone
What the Soul has left undone
And which three of them cannot do
And have left undone
The Head (Ori) has been doing it
Silently, confidently, diligently

## My Sustainer–2

I pay homage to Air
For sustaining me without a word of gratitude
I pay home to Water
For sustaining me without a word of gratitude
I pay home to Earth
For sustaining me without a word of gratitude

I called upon the Air
To make the Earth healthful
I invited the Water to enrich the Earth
I called upon the sun to ripen it

The Air, the Water, the Earth
Are faithfully sustaining me
Without a word of gratitude
Why should I forget to be grateful?
Do I know how to convert my ingratitude
Into gratitude?
Yes, I do.
Consequently, I count myself a good friend of
The Air, the Earth and the Water
My indispensable sustainers!!!

## Why So Many Fires in the World

**(A Dialogue Betwixt Yemi and His Alter ego)**
A rat-a-tat-tat was heard on my front door
I rushed out with a bucket of water
Thinking I had to douse the fire attacking
The roof of my shed.

**Yemi:** Are you the one knocking
During this crepuscular hours of the gloaming?
**My alter ego:** "Yes," said my alter ego,
Laughing humorously
**Yemi:** Is the world safe?
**Alter ego:** What do you mean?
**Yemi:** Is the humanity safe?
**Alter ego:** Yes, we are safe.

**Yemi:** Why do you say we are safe?
When the four corners of the world
Are guarded by fires
Not less fiery than conflagrations?
**Alter-ego:** I know what you are driving at
It is true that the four corners of the world
Are heavily guarded. If the Animal Kingdom
Could guard their territory with what they have
Humans should be able to guard themselves.

**Yemi:** I am scared to see me surrounded
By fatal fires of machete, axes, tomahawks
Guns, bombs, missiles and nuclear weapons
It shouldn't be that way, Oh God
I feel like retreating to my original habitat
And stay there till the trashing of these weapons
Till the fires surrounding
The four corners of the world are extinguished
Until man moves from nadir to the zenith.

**Alter-ego:** Well said: womb, the original home
Of every man born of woman is a place to ensconce

**Yemi:** Why is it that man is so scared
To live sans fear and suspicion?

**Alter ego:** We fail to develop passion for Nature
Good Nature: indispensable, genesis of everything
We misuse Nature that inspires us as artists
We forget to recognize that art is the expression
And cultivation of interest in Nature
Instead of promoting Nature in its purity
We promote weaponry, detrimental to Nature
As we destroy Nature, we destroy ourselves!

**Yemi:** All these man-made fires
The reason why man deflated of peace?

**Alter ego:** Man cannot have peace
When man is fearful of peace.

**Yemi:** Is it true to say that a genuine love is lacking?

**Alter ego:** Yes. A genuine love: it's like desideratum.

**Yemi:** How can we find the genuine love?

**Alter ego:** All those anti-Nature weaponry
Must be replaced by passion for Nature of life
Then, it is only then the fires will stop burning

**Yemi:** All these fires, all these fears
Are assailing humanity because we are
Overtaken by a defeat of reason? Correct?

**Alter-ego:** Correct, absolutely.

**Yemi:** Oh from your Ori, cometh enlightenment, always
And this ken, I will bruit abroad
To the four corners of the planet.

*My Queen-Wife, supposed*
*To be sleeping and snoring*
*Like a Queen-Mother, overheard*
*Our conversation and said, "It is not enough*
*To stop fires from utterly destroying the earth*
*We must also do everything possible*
*To prevent their outbreaks."*

## Life, A Miracle

Born to a moment
Schooled by a moment
Began to learn from a moment
By my graduation
I've known that Life is a miracle.

*A Dream,*
*Life, garbed in*
*Unconsciousness*
*Life, a Dream garbed in*
*Consciousness*

What I see that are visible
What I can't see that are invisible
All sustained by Nature, defined by Nature
As I reminisced about the mythical
And non-mythical phenomena.

I begin to realize, to comprehend
That Life is a miracle
Bound in unison with Death
And garbed in the inscrutability
Of Creator-Philosopher Olodumare.

## The Unseasonable Hour

When curiosity lured me
To the sepulcher of my pedigrees
Where kola-nuts are gathered
From the thorns

Where grains of paradise are gathered
From the thistles
Where I realized that my ancestors
Are glutted with peace of mind

The unseasonable hour
Where my eyes filled with a passion of tears
And deportment. Where my curiosity
Amidst tranquil contemplations, interred sempiternally.

## First World Words on Inter-racial Marriage

Will you love me the way I am?
I will. I will. I will
Will you ever dump me?
Because of my hue?
No. I will deport myself with dignity
Or else Mother Nature will punish me
If ever I think of doing so

Then hug me, love me
Cuddle me, charm me, and ennoble me
Let's breathe this
Zephyr of compassion
Let our eyes draw tears of compassion
For those who could not cross
The bridge like us.

Now give me
A passion fruit to munch
And a cup of living water to sip
And a rose to regale with gusto
An a ring to cherish
And let me lay this my head
Upon your loving heart.

Let us rejoice and be glad
In Creator-Philosopher Olodumare for opening
The doors of our hearts
To the first world words
Leading to the charity of inter-racial marriage
Under the calm strength of love
That knows neither borders nor hues.

## My First Prayer in 21st Century

In this day and age
This, modern day and age
My supplications to Creator-Philosopher Olodumare
To open my eyes, my ears, my hands
My power to smell, my power to taste
So as to see, hear, touch, smell and taste
Like the creators, the makers
The Thought Men and Women
Using their ori–heads
In this day and age.

## I Don't Want To End Up . . .

I don't want to end up
Simply visiting this world
I want to pour upon the earth

Modicums of holy water
Ere the earth opens up to swallow me
To my chagrin and disconsolation

Coming back, on my coming back
I will change those modicums of holy water
Into a holy beginning in a paradisiacal world, worldly.

## Kill the Tragic Lure

If only I could assail the wisdom
Of the Thought Men and Women
The tragic lure would be killed
With the aid of our ancestors/pedigrees

Now ensconcing in harmony
In their second domicile
Entertaining no fear to killing the tragic lure
But to lure and love, sempiternally.

**Inspired and Aspired**

Kids, my kids, you've been inspired
By what is known
Even by what is unknown

In order to aspire after knowledge
From all the four corners of the world, worldly
My largesse for you

As you carve your identities
Based on **Inspiration**
An **Aspiration**.

## Living in Peace and Content

I have no status symbols
To my credit
Nothing do I have
That can add to your heart's content
But I have something else
That will enable you
To live in peace and content
That would make you content
Till the end of your life
Your everlasting gift.

## B-E-A-U-T-Y

Beautiful community (**B** and **B**), mine, thine, ours
Bedecked with aesthetic colors, colorful
And the artistic beauty, beautiful
Thine radiance, sunflower, enthralls me, seizes me captive
Sunflower, thine seeds planted, deeply rooted
Thine resilience magical, wondrous, baffles me
Thine radiance charms me inescapably
Permit me to hug you with tears of joys in my eyes
Ere setting my feet upon the stones of the pathway
My feet quickening: guided by the rays of your beauty.

If beauty epitomizes artworks & vice versa
I seek and find beauty in all artistic works and virtuosity
Let that beautify our community
With decorative arts, eyeful, growing, glowing
And say loud and clear, of all the aesthetic things
On the surface of the earth and under the vault of heaven
None is as beautiful as the beautiful art-rainbow
When I look at you, your Ola Oshun-like beauty arrests me
When I touch you, I touch the beauty-goddess in you
Created in the spitting image of Creator-Philosopher
   Olodumare.

Sunflower, thine beauty a work of art
It's like magic, magicking, dovetailing with a charity of love
Thine characteristics inimitable
Sometimes thine beauty is like a scherzando
Sometimes it strengthens my imagination
By sharpening its delicacy and
By enlarging its ranges, purviews and nuances
Thou art a generous gift to our community/humanity
This poem, my votive tribute/sacrifice to your beauty
That I and others may live peacefully, happily like
    the immortality.

Beauty, can I adore you like I adore the curative sea breeze?
Like I adore the Queen of beauty, Queen Ola Oshun
Like my ever beautiful and radiant sunflower
Beauty, thou hast personalized Queen Ola Oshun
Let me lay my forlorn heart upon your heart,
Upon your flower-bedecked pillow
And see myself transported into a beautiful sleep
Inundated with romantic, sweet and perfumery dreams
While offering you a flower suffused with nectar, my sunflower
That never withers, always kissing the sun's rays.


Transitioning from beauty to pulchritude
I graduated to the status of beau ideal
Gratitude, appreciation, a bond of affection

My food for contentment and beauty, beautiful
My beauty giving back to our community of children

Beauty analogous to peace, respect and happiness, sculpted
Found in the way my correspondence smiles betwixt young and old
In the way I philosophically read and write
In the way I dress and greet beauty, beautiful
In the way my organic, delicious food, munched and sipped

Beauty, give me thine magic of youthful exuberance
I want to cherish you till the end of time
Come to me and stay with me poetizing
Thine magic makes you meaningful and attractive, always
Beauty, you're a winner, a prayer, a religion, a fate prevailed.

                                    (**B** and **B**==Black and Brown)

## Boston–A City of Sisterly Love

I looked upon the spherical hill
Behold humanity rejoicing upon the Beacon Hill
A sisterly love born, 1971
I looked upon the spherical stamping ground
Behold humanity dancing on the City Hall Plaza
A sisterly love born, 1985

Then a yodel of celebration, pervaded Boston-scope
Seeing the clock ticking
Seeing the hourglass measuring time
By trickling: not only a fund of humor?
Also a fund of happiness, affirmed poetically
As two sisters (one after the other) **M&M**

Extolling the practice of love
Made Boston a **City of Sisterly Love**
Would this suit the book of the literary community?
Each sister whose first name starts with letter **M**
Shining in the glitter of the moonlight
Likened to the first gleams of the morning sun
Witnessing the first but one city, a **City of Sisterly Love**

I gleefully doffed my spherical hat to the duo democrats
Domiciling in a city where culture elevates
Where art, thou a marvel of ingenuity, symbol of reality

Entranced, I, in their calm strength of intellectual
And artistic virtuosity, meritoriously
Mirthfully, I pirouetted to the music of the spheres!

# PART THREE

## The Star of Enlightenment

(That Illuminates Within Us)

**Introduction**

**The Star of Enlightenment** was on the last leg of completion when the death of a nonagenarian Nelson Mandela was announced in December of 2013. Poetically, the Star of Enlightenment is an exploration into the divine sacrifice offered to elicit the wheels of thoughts, impacted by alphabetical letters that stand for names of persons and names of all the fields of knowledge and learning. It contains all the alphabetically arranged letters (A-Z) from which you and I will find the first letters of our names, as well as the first letters of the names of our deity-ancestors, one of whom now is Nelson Mandela. There is no name of any human being treading upon the surface of this earth without his or her first letter-name being captured, represented, alphabetized, sung or immortalized by a letter in this poetry book, first of its kind. It is true to assert that man must have pronounced, read or met all the persons bearing all those letters in a lifetime. Like other publications before it, **The Star of Enlightenment** recognizes our deity-ancestors (especially in Yoruba worldview) as divinity-philosophers. The Star of Enlightenment recognizes every human being as a star, searching and treading the Way of Enlightenment. But the Way of Enlightenment that is being illuminated by the Star of Enlightenment could, many a time be rough, brutal, inhuman, cruel, barbaric, racist, ungodly and treacherous. No wonder that only a few is able to find and possess the Star of Enlightenment, the ultimate goal of every human being seeking the Way of Enlightenment. This book lets us follow, letter by letter how to look for, and possess this all-purpose, all-divine, all-desirable supernova of enlightenment that is created to illuminate our lives, courtesy of Creator-Philosopher Olodumare/God.

**Prefatory Light**

Perceptively, the star of enlightenment is a philosophical star that radiates from the Yoruba Book of Enlightenment. Whosoever finds and owns the star finds and owns a good thing in life. Once found, and possessed, it is a panacea, a cure-all to anything that may derail our smiling happiness or our beatific felicity.

**Ori** (head) is everything in life as mathematics is everything in life. A head is the definition of the body, giving meaning to all the parts of the body as mathematics (no matter how rudimentary it is) gives meaning to everything we do. On a daily basis, is there anything we can do without addition, subtraction, multiplication and division? The answer is a monosyllabic No.

Said philosopher Reuben O. Ogunyemi, "Philosophically, everyone is hungry and ireful. But only those who can manage and bury their ire and solve their hunger are the happy and smiling ones. They are the ones who can share their love and live a married life."

All the twenty-six letters in the English alphabet, which are in this poetry book emanate from the head, the custodian of our destinies. They represent all the known fields of learning or knowledge, which will not be possible without the head and without the knowledge of addition, subtraction, multiplication and division standing on the shoulders of Mathematics. The Way of Enlightenment, lighted by the star is the answer to any questions we may have on happiness, beauty, love and healthy life.

One thing we must remember and conceptualize is that a newborn does not know the date of its birth. In other words, which should be highlighted as a matter of fact, no one knows his or her date of birth until he or she is told during the years of innocence. At this stage of life, the right name that will epitomize peace, success and happiness is very vital. In order to ensure that one possesses a good head from infancy, one's destiny through one's head must be sought. Once sought and known and accepted, no one could coerce you into doing something from outside the realm of your destiny or doing something if that something is against what your head (ori) has destined for you

Due to the signification of the head, everything created moves in a circle. For example, human beings are created in circles of life. When we die, leaving the physical world, we follow a circle and come back in a circle. The world endures forever. In another way of rephrasing it, what goes around comes around. See the rain, it comes from the clouds and goes back to the clouds—in circles. The water we drink, the food we eat, come from the earth and go back to the earth in circles.

The fire burns in circles. The currents of the river move in circles. The moon phases in circles. The sun rises and when it sets, it goes back to its source in a circle, while the earth is doing its business of rotation. Winds blow in circles. Love is made in circles. Sands of time are in circles. Trees and hills are formed in circles. The weathers obey the circles of seasons. News spread in circles. Human beings associate in circles; hence we have business circles or a circle of friends.

**Dedication−1**

To Chief Obafemi Awolow (the first premier of Western Nigeria) for his pragmatic idealism that led to the building of the first Radio and TV Houses in Africa. His idea also led to the first Cocoa House in the world, and the first modern stadium in Africa, called Liberty Stadium.

## Dedication–2

To Nelson Mandela, for being the only revolutionary and hero of a human being in the nonfictional history of mankind to be imprisoned for twenty-seven years, awarded Nobel Prize for Peace, became the President of his beloved country and turned racial disharmony into a global LOVE, through the divine grace and benevolence of our loving omnipresent Creator-Philosopher God/Olodumare.

## Dedication–3

To Wole Soyinka for his eloquent and powerful Nobel Speech, "This Past Must Address Its Present," delivered in 1986 while accepting his Nobel Prize in Literature Award, and for his book, "Mandela's Earth and Other Poems," published in 1989. The Nobel Speech as well as the poetry book touched the world's hearts of hearts, and months later, Nelson Mandela walked into freedom of a free world, sandwiched betwixt sanity and insanity, in 1990.

**Dedication—4**

Dedicated to President Barack Obama for his audacity, his pragmatism, his transparency: and for his passion for all the peoples (particularly the middle class) of the United States and the rest of the world. The stamp of ingenuity on his physiognomy makes him an incarnate of the long-awaited Son of Man.

## Dedication—5

To Divinity-Philosopher Oduduwa for being the Bringer of Light to the Yoruba people, worldwide, for being the pioneer and the father of Yoruba Philosophy, that lets us know that ori—head is the definition of the body and the substrate unto which other parts of the body are answerable.

**Dedication-6**

Dedicated to the political-cum-religious-philosopher Martin Luther King Junior for sacrificing his precious life for us to relish the calm strength of human rights and American dreams.

# PART FOUR

## Chief Awo's Exceeding Joy, 1959

## Inaugurating the First Television Service in Africa

A noble hero: smitten with noble ambitions
Amongst the nobilities
Shall dwell no more in the dark
In informing and educating our people.

**WNTV, October 31st 1959**, the ladder
To climb to the greater heights
As we strive for the best
In the history of this country.

Tune on your radio and television sets
Telling us, if Africa shall rise
Shall rise with every big idea
Idealized, realized and exemplified.

Effusive and pleased, I am, to let you know
My idea, born out of exuberating imaginations
A new day, dawned fair
As stagnation interred.

Joyful, elated, hurrah!
The birth of radio and TV journalism
Instrumental to our mass education
Born palpable, in this unprepossessing city of Ibadan.

In this unprepossessing city of Ibadan
Capital of the Western Nigeria
Dubbed a land
Flowing with milk and honey.

Africa, arise
Arise with the much-needed ideas
Big and transparent ideas
Needed, on our way to the acme of Olumo rocks.

## Post Independence

Granted my dream of big ideas, oh Olodumare
Reality in fullness brought
Let's nurture and foster
This dream, novel, born.

A beginning of new light
Lit in the middle
Of the 20th century, weary
Weary of anxieties, negotiations and tribulations.

The fire of progress
Never to be extinguished
The independence flag
Hoisted, ne'er to be lowered.

As we confront our challenges
Smooth and rough realities
We never shall give up
And relapse in complacency.

Spiritually and physically
Here, hear a call, a patriotic call
Shall be answered
As we are sure bent.

On working with cardinal virtues
Love, morality, honor, honesty, bravery
Temperance, justice, prudence and fortitude
Emblematic of good leadership.

Here, the edifice of success, stay
Till eternity like our celestial star
As we progress toward
One Nigeria, with vim and victory.

# PART FIVE

## My Goal In Life
## (My Crown of Jewels)

Goodness me, what is my goal in life? (This is the same question my father once asked. As a chip of the old block, it is incumbent on me to ask the same question). Can the head please tell me what my goal is? It is being divined that my destiny lies in my head. And my head (ori) has let me know that my goal is to find my Star of Enlightenment that will take me to the Way of Enlightenment lined by the twenty-six alphabets. The twenty-six English alphabets are the names of human beings. They belong to males and females in the global human community. Happily, I see some of them, e-mail some of them, talk to some of them, and read about some of them on a daily basis. Each one of us has been destined to play a part in the global human community, for the destined human existence is committed to many registers of harmony, rhythm, melody, and it is not given to anyone to play all of them.

**A:**

Awaking with a stretch and a yawn
Found lying before me
A ball of starry light
Beckoning to me
With an infectious smile

Abundance is my cup of hope
Thus I started to plan a move
Moving to grasp the star
With might and main
Rain or shine.

**B:**

Beaten by the inclement weather
Knocked down by vicissitudes of life
Bludgeoned and bruised
Nonetheless I vowed to grasp my star
As long as Creator-Philosopher Olodumare lives

Hearing the sound of my footsteps
Segueing alphabetically
As I raced towards my star
Of enlightenment
Jazzing with wit and wisdom.

## C:

Comestible, I have none
But hope, I have in abundance
Ready to uplift me to life
For life and hope have teamed up together
And my success assured

Consequential is my capital idea
The idea that I must pursue and take
The star of my enlightenment
And then rejoice gratefully
In the name of Creator-Philosopher God.

**D:**

Destiny has positioned my footsteps
With determination in place
There is no going back
I must grasp what's mine
And then rejoice eternally

Diamond-driven, yes I am diamond-driven
By all the sinews of my energy
My energy will never sap
My focus is strong
And will remain strong and serious.

**E:**

Energized, I am
Emboldened, I am
My shanks are ready
My soles are ready
My spirit, uplifted as ever

Enlightened, I want to be
And here is the time to do just that
My vision has come to stay
And here is the scenario
Of my itineraries.

**F:**

Fortitude, yes. Forward ever
Backward never
My shanks are ready
My head, the definition of my body
To see me through.

For what is good for the goose
Is good for the gander
What is good to chew
Is good to swallow
Swallowing without borborygmus.

**G:**

Gosh, my gold: the star is smart
Playing the game of elusiveness
But I will never give up
For I am a winner
That never quits

Good to remain alert
Good to be optimistic
Step by step, day by day
I'll race after mine, as valuable as a gold medal
And my valuable will soon be mine forever.

**H:**

Head, my head will bring me happiness
It is going to be a divine happiness
Divine happiness my pursuit
It is my prize, gold
It is my fortune

Head, thou my happiness will bring
The star of happiness belongs to my head
The star of enlightenment is my head
And I promise to grasp my star
That's mine, my head and destiny forever.

**I:**

Interesting to know that
The star of enlightenment
Illuminating my head
My soul, my heart, my mind
The star, mine, sooner than expected

Illuminate me, thou star
That ne'er quenches
A song that uplifts me
That I will tearfully sing
Till my star starts to shine upon me.

**J:**

Just before me
Are the judges of the day
Judging in my favor
The need for me to have
A star of enlightenment

Justice is mine, hurrah
I am free to grasp
My destiny anytime, any day
For time is the factor
And it is on my side.

**K:**

Knowledge may elude me
If procrastination rears its ugly head
To own and cherish
The star of enlightenment
Needed by all human beings.

Knowledge needed, not wanted
It will be permanent
Knowledge that knows no barriers
That illuminates the entire world
Like the star of enlightenment.

**L:**

Love, is there any one I can boast of?
Surely, I have more than enough
I think my love can cure any forlorn hope
If only I can possess my ankh-like star
Of aura and enlightenment

Living a positive life
Showing others how positive I am
Ideal for the star of enlightenment
That shines on me
That makes the world divine.

**M:**

Metaphysics will be replaced
By idealism vis-à-vis realism
Yielding to an absolute determinism
The rationale behind my running after
An everlasting illumination.

Methodology is but indispensable
In pursuing and overtaking my objective
The ankh-like star my objective
It may run as fast as a cheetah
But it cannot hide like the hand of invisibility.

**N:**

No one can stop me from achieving my ambition
Save Creator-Philosopher God/Olodumare
But Creator-Philosopher Olodumare/God
Would be inundated with ingredients of happiness
If I could achieve my ambition

Nose-diving or head-long, falling
I will never quit
For what's worth doing
Is worth doing well
The right thing, I've done, setting out at dawn.

**O:**

Occasionally, I may stumble
And bark up the wrong tree
Nevertheless, my path is being prepared
Smooth by Divinity-Philosopher Ogun
The artificer of all metallic things

Oblation, is it the next thing?
No, I don't think so
I need the supplications of our Divinity-Philosophers
Who are versed in the destiny of ori–head
And who will light my way.

## P:

Philosophy: it's said, antecedent to religion
But how can I make use of either of them?
Without the courtesy of ori–head
Who is the definition of the body, the substrate
Unto which other parts of the body are answerable to

Putting it simply, my head–ori
Will lead me to where my star is
Waiting for me, while running like a cheetah
What I need is to quicken my paces
So that my goal is reached.

**Q:**

Quintessential is my goal
There is no compromise
No surprise
No distraction
My star of enlightenment is what I need

Questions may be asked
If and when questions are asked
My rejoinder, divine and simple
I need to be illuminated
By the star of enlightenment.

**R:**

Repertoire of songs, but respecting others
During this spiritual race, vital
I will play my part with fairness
As demanded by every competition
Are competitors hundred percent fair?

Rarely fair, my answer
But mine, a different kind of competition
Stars, plenty enough for every individual
Requirements are simple
Be on the trot, run and never quit.

**S:**

Sublime is the star of enlightenment
The race for sublimity has begun in earnest
Racing after an ankh-like star
Along the sublime way
Of enlightenment

Serendipity may want to seduce me
But I need to be wary
And if I stumble and fall
I will look back to determine
The reason or cause for my stumble.

**T:**

Thoughtful towards my future
I must be on the qui vive
For upon what my eyes have been set
I will own it and no other star
Shall be bigger than what I have owned

To one and all
I promise to bring home
A star, this ankh-like star
The passion of my life
The illumination and the blessings upon A-Z.

**U:**

Understanding the spiritual language
To claim what's mine in line with my destiny
It's fundamental to my head—ori
For it is my destiny
To obtain the star of enlightenment

Under no circumstances: under no illusion
Shall I trade my ambition with triviality
For my words,
As for my unspoken words
Are final, courtesy of Creator-Philosopher God

## V:

Valor, to the house of valorous men and women
Prayerful is my house
With prayers, we should all find what is ours
Through the benevolence of our heads
The crowns of all the parts of our bodies

Verisimilitude is almost as dependable
As morality, one of the cardinal virtues
In Yoruba culture
Thus my journey has become
A task that must be done.

**W:**

Wit and wisdom
Needed to my Way of Enlightenment
I will long for both
Both grow inside the star of enlightenment
I claim them: they are mine

Wellness is another reason
And the reasons are numerous
They are good for something reasons
Reasons that make one smile
Reasons that radiate happiness.

**X:**

Xylophone; let me dance to you
I will sing my favorite lilt
Knowing that my success is nigh
Gosh, with perseverance
My success is nigh and inevitable.

Xenophobia, you have been defeated
From all the paths of rationality
Thou art the backburner of barbarity
Barriers to cultures broken
Thou road: you will never be my driver again.

## Y:

Yammering, no: not my style nor my character
Subscribes only to a divine and uplifting milieu
The distance is becoming shorter and shorter
The **Way of Enlightenment**, congrats, is reached
And my ankh-like star has accomplished its mission

Yodeling for happiness and exuberance
Leaping for joy and Pollyannaism
Singing, come to me all ye people
Good things are beginning to happen in my life
Come one, come all!

**Z:**

Zenith, to the zenith, philosophically
I am lifted higher and higher
As I grabbed my star in my hand, the star
That has led me to the Way of Enlightenment
My star of enlightenment: my illumination.

Zealous for immortal love
Zealous for divine happiness and peace
The treasure of a lifetime, my crown of jewels
Can we now exceedingly rejoice?
Let's rejoice, dine and wine, reaching the top of my bent.

# PART SIX

# The Nine Cardinal Virtues of the Yoruba Folk Philosophy

The world is created out of unconditional love. Thus the Yoruba people believe that whosoever cannot love himself to love others has a broken destiny. The nine cardinal virtues (fortitude, honesty, honor, justice, love, morality, prudence, temperance and valor) in Yoruba culture are the guidelines for the Yoruba people. These virtues (as poetized below) are to be found in their folk philosophy, as well as in their prophetic religion.

**Fortitude:**

See my courage as being firm
See me displaying patient endurance
Of sorrows and misfortunes

My physical strength, indeed my physique
Will not be mine without fortitude
Can resist any physical and spiritual attack.

## Honesty:

Fairness is my passionate friend
Integrity, my own, is like my preceptor
Probity, my own, is like my neighbor

Inviting purity to join me
Inviting sincerity, uprightness and rectitude
To be my witness, if God is my eye-witness.

**Honor:**

Honor me as you see me
As I perch resplendently
On the Throne of Grace

I will treat you with dignity
You will reciprocate with a feeling of camaraderie
With your reputation and good name.

Justice: Don't be too judgmental
If you do, remember to apply justice
And be fair within your heart and your soul

In the name of fairness,
I will endeavor to be wary
For being righteous is my daily endearment.

**Love:**

Love me as you promise to
Love yourself so that you can love me
Let your love be divine and infectious

I will divine my love to be strong
Infectious physically and spiritually
Blessing both of us with sweet dreams.

## Morality:

Moralize me ceaselessly—day and night
I need your snippets of morality
To be part and parcel of my growing

Righteousness affects character
And character, incomplete without righteousness
Thus I need both to be my alter egos.

**Prudence:**

If and when it comes to the crunch
Whenever I elect to be a gentleman
Prudence will elect to be my second nature

Prudence is my char of lemon tea
In my Throne of Grace, sipped in modicums
With sheer deliberation and discretion.

**Temperance:**

Temperance, good for one and all
I claim it diametrically
Its essence is juicy and everlasting

In moderation, I box myself
My front door bears a sign of abstinence
No one can tempt me nor will I tempt anyone.

**Valor:**

My valor has defeated fear wherever fear is found
Valor is a catch-phrase on the lips of heroes and heroines
Of this present generation

Valor will be passed to the next generation
For there will be no room for chicken-hearted men
And their counterparts, if Creator-Olodumare is my witness.

# PART SEVEN

## Chasing a Mare's Nest

The Night has played its part
With all its nocturnal propensities
And the Day has begun to itemize
Its own diurnal propensities
This is the circle of life shared betwixt
Day and Night. It goes on without fail
For it is the destiny betwixt the Day and Night

Argumentatively, the Day is the head
The Night serves as the tail
The Day is the opposite of the Night
The Night is the antonym of the Day
Both of them display the aesthetic contradictions
Always found in every creature in life.

The hours of the night had passed. It was a rainy day
 of unsettled weathers when the **Body** said
to the **Head**, "I will like to go and find the tallest iroko tree,
 climb it to the topmost and see
how beautiful the world is. Whatever I discover or
 experience, I will bring it back to you."
"You mean you want to leave without me?"
 asked the **Head**.
"Yes, I just want to be free once in a lifetime and discover
 the world by myself."
"This is but unusual."

"I know but I want to set a record or rather a precedent."

"Your quest is like a mare's nest. Well, go ahead. But remember that it is not your destiny to do anything without me. Your destiny resides in me," said the **Head**, knitting his brows and disfiguring his lips with a moue.

Having had the road cleared and sanctified by Divinity-Philosopher Ogun, so that the road might not attempt to be his driver, he set out. On reaching the precincts of a virgin forest whose trees are largely stunted, it dawned on him that he would be ridiculed or mocked as a goblin or as a monster without a head. In this respect, he said he had to talk to some of the creatures in the forest. On seeing an elephant, he implored him to lend him his head. The elephant laughed and told him that his head was so stone-heavy that he would not be able to move an inch if he had to carry it. A few yards later, he saw an orangutan. After explaining to him his mission, the primate lent him his head. His was happy, whistling hilariously.

On reaching the middle of the forest, he met a dendrologist who showed him where to find the tall iroko trees. Sooner than expected, he found a very tall iroko tree. He tried three times to climb it to the top but he could not because the bole of the tree was so slippery due to the rain. Knowing that he was at his wit's end, he was ireful and crestfallen.

The rain had let up by the time he got home having giving back to orangutan his head. Still looking crestfallen, he proceeded to relate the futility of his adventure to the **Head**, ori.

Chortling and hiccoughing, the **Head** said to him, "Don't you know that I, the **Head** is the definition of the **Body**, the substrate unto which all the parts of the Body are answerable?"

Looking at his boss, he apologetically said, "Now I know you are my boss whose destiny is more propitious than mine and I will never again do anything without you."

In both prophetic and proverbial words, the **Head** said, "I saw all what happened to you during your mare's nest. My eyes may be small but my heart is big. Because my heart is big, I can hear you talking even if I close my small eyes. You see, destiny is a very strange phenomenon. It asks for everything and lures everybody to fall within its design or domain. One must serve him like a master. As a matter of fact, which can not be disputed beyond the premise of rationale, he is a master with a passé-partout, and everyone else is his servant."

# PART EIGHT

## A Classic Poem for Nelson Mandela

### (Truth and Reconciliation)

Destined to be great, albeit a humble beginning
While taking the rough with the smooth
Fighting for justice and equality
In his beloved country of grains of paradise
But the workers of apartheid, on discovering the
Grains of paradise refused to see the star of justice.

Imprisoned for raising his voice of justice
The civilized world playing double game
As long as the grains of paradise
Available enriching the workers of the apartheid
While the natives moan in apartheid-made slavery

A land flowing with milk and honey
Suddenly, a terrorist, they stigmatized him
Let's keep him there, for if released from jail
He will scoop the grains from our bowls and platters
And set the country on an unquenchable fire

But to us a child has been born
A child breathing like the Son of Man
Thou shall kill his body, said the prophecy
But thou shall not kill his soul, said the prophecy
Alas, no one knew the Son of Man
Until shown by Creator-Philosopher Olodumare

Gosh, the world is a theatre, alas
Of good and bad, of bright and dark
But he had chosen nothing less than the good
Upholding his personal philosophy of love
The treasure of a lifetime, upshot of happiness
One such a philosopher in a million.

Certainly, Creator-Philosopher God/Olodumare
Does not slumber or sleep
With Poetry such as Mandela's Earth, with speeches,
Demonstrations, protests, writings, prayers
    and supplications
Mandela was set free after 27 fat years! Free at last
Rightfully, he found the Way of Enlightenment waiting




Hurrah, the stone abandoned at the stygian corner
Has become the **center** of the house
Awarded Nobel Peace Prize
Became the President of his beloved country

And died a hero, an anointed prince of peace
With a Star of Enlightenment as his personal halo

Rest in perfect peace oh Madiba Mandela
Now that the tree of love you've planted by the
Riverside has started **fruiting love and forgiveness**
(The aesthetic to which you are faithful)
As you start your divine journey
With the Star and the Book of Enlightenment
To the domain of our ancestors.

## A Classic Poem for Wole Soyinka

### (This Past Must Address Its Present)
Your literary voice, an international
A wake-up call since 1962
With your unprecedented Telephone Conversation
Here is the irony, inevitable
Months later, Mandela imprisoned?

Following the catalogues of ironies
Nobel Prize in literature awarded
And your voice more trenchant
Recounting the catalogues of injustices
In a civilized world of savants and thinkers

But the love in your histrionic voice,
Comprehends the way the cookie crumbles
Commenced, caressing the hearts of the world
With your eloquent Nobel Speech in 1986
Together with love of Creator-Philosopher Olodumare
Your friend, Mandela set free in 1990!

## A Classic Poem for Barack Obama

**(There's only One United States of America)**
Your way, a propitious one
Cleared and sanctified by Divinity-Philosopher Ogun
Here, on the tessellated Way of Enlightenment
This, you've found with the Star
And the Book of Enlightenment

Your voice of justice and equality
I have heard on many occasions
Yearning for ethnical and racial equalities
On political, economic, educational
And social imprints, under the vault of heaven

From Abuja, Accra, Berlin, Cairo, Johannesburg,
London, New Delhi, Paris, Washington, DC to . . .
Your voice, calling for justice
Dinning justice, one of the nine cardinal virtues
Lodestar in the quintessence worn as dashikis
Around the Yoruba folk philosophy.

## Author's Spiritual Hole

In this **spot**, tiny as an ant's hole
Here Decision of Life and Death made
Happiness my lot, though.

Having defeated Death and its agents
In my joyful moments
I've leaped towards the star of immortality.

I am striving towards the best star of immortality
The best as observed keenly in Nature
In all these years of my unmarked **spot**.

I do not, cannot claim perfection
Yet perfection is my ultimate goal
In my quest for the star of sublimity–spiritual

Many times I have heartily burnt my finger
If I ever burn my finger again
I need you–blowing a soothing air to it.

Even if you have no finger to burn
I may one day be there for you in your **spot**
When you, in your unconditional love, crave for.

Either way, the Spiritual Creator-Philosopher
    God/Olodumare
Keeps telling me that ere man his potential reaches
He must undergo some pain—some finger-burning.

## One Third a Writer

One Third a Writer I would love to be
Lucubrating without ceasing
In search of my whole self.

Of pain of writing pregnant
The birth, the joy of having written
Becoming the charity of humanity.

Even when the way
The cookie crumbles explicitly known
Mine, onus to find out

Why my feet are touching the ground
Whereas my legs in the air still dangling
Still many rivers to cross.

## The Leki Massacre of 10/20/2020

Perennial—The failed Government comes
The failed Government goes
Starting from the massacre during the civil war
The histrionic events
The End-SARS peaceful protesters

Fatally brutalized by the Nigerian army
Ticked with killings
Ticked with shameful and preposterous acts
Youths in their hundreds
Yodeling, leaderlessly

Let my people go
The failed government
Guilty to the kilt
Out of kilter, irredeemable
The histrionic events

Ticked with numerous killings
Ticked with shameful and preposterous acts
The failed government comes
The failed government goes
Pointing to many **adventurous students**

Some perished in the Sahara Desert
Some perished upon the Mediterranean Sea
Some in Diaspora, perished
While on the trot, scraping a living
Away from the failed government comes

The failed government goes
The over 200 linguistic ethnic tongues/groups
Now waking up
Enlightening now, they are
Forming their own peaceful nation-states

As they shun the amalgamated geography
**The Lekki massacre of October 20, 2020**
Is another fire amongst fires
Set by the Boko Haram
And the herdsmen killing with impunity

The geography, a byword for retardation?
The historic present, bearing it out
Summation of the *zeitgeist*
A pointer to the putrefied retardation
While the present inanition cannot
Be ignored. But the *zeitgeist,*
Fully comprehended
**One massacre, too many.**

## Our Ancestors Have Spoken!!!
### For R-E-P-A-R-A-T-I-O-N-S

    Slavery, condemned—brutality, unsurpassed
Stealing, buying and selling human beings
By the fortune makers

Our ancestors aggrieved
Have spoken, lung power, in favor of
R-E-P-A-R-A-T-I-O-N-S

Honoring reparations
Honoring LOVE over and above racism
Hailing the world yearning for peace

For many years, jumping gaps of
Of prejudices and racisms
Enough is enough, O Olodumare!

For you and me—reparations—NOW
Our ancestors peacefully yelling
Peacefully yelling for so many years!!!

## Fait accompli (The Epilogue)

Here fait accompli is imbued with recapitulation. As mentioned in the Introduction and in the Prefatory Light, The Star of Enlightenment is being illuminated by both the poetic and the philosophical ambivalence. From A-Z, it has been a tough journey that's always taking the rough with the smooth like the vicissitudes of life. Thus fait accompli evidences the fact that the poetic vis-à-vis the philosophical journey is a success and that success should not be reversed.

Every movement from one point to another is a journey according to Yoruba folk philosophy. In this wise, we make journeys or go on journeys every blessed day. In order to be on the safer side of our journeys, Divinity-philosopher Ogun is invariably preparing the way/road for us so that the road will never attempt to become our driver.

Additionally, everyone that makes, or goes on a journey is a planner, courtesy of ori—head. Professionally perceived, that means we need to plan in order to stay fit and focused at the helm of our callings. This is how philosopher Chief Awo put it, "Those who desire to reach, and keep their places at the top in any calling must be prepared to do so the hard way." This lets us know that we must be ready to face the smooth and the rough whenever we plan to do anything in life: just anything and everything humane to be done, under the vault of heaven, in this mortal world, worldly. In sum, planning to go on a journey can be likened to planning for one's calling. Each one of us has to play a part in this beautiful, global human community, for the destined human existence is committed to many registers and it is not given to anyone to play all of them.

## Author Bio:

**About the Author:** Former research fellow, Harvard University, former Director, Institute of Creative Writing, author of The Aesthetic and Moral Art of Wole Soyinka, Yoruba Idealism, and a good few; recipient of a Poetry Golden Trophy, recipient of the 2021 Nonfiction Fellowship Award from the Writers' Room of Boston, recipient of the 2023 Humanities Grant from the Massachusetts Cultural Council, Yemi D. Ogunyemi (also known as Yemi D. Prince) is an aphorist and a luminous literary philosopher whose work reflects the savvies and radiance of his spirit, and always fascinated by letters, books and the power of words. His corpora which is a blend of Yoruba folk philosophy, autochthonous religion and literature, is purposed to inform, enlighten, educate, entertain, inspire and above all, inoculate the body with the ingredients of wellness and happiness. While he believes that good literature adds fullness to the meaning of life, he also believes that art, the marvel of ingenuity, a symbol of reality, is an expression of happiness, an application of human creative skill. To date, Yemi has authored over seventy titles of literary works–fiction, nonfiction, plays, poetry and children's stories. His most recent work is Yoruba Idealism. His eBooks include The World, in a Fume of Pandemic Anxiety, Quid Pro Quo and Other Narratives and How to Erase Racism from the Minds of Humanity. Currently, he is working on The Study of Yoruba Classic Fairytales/Folklore and Literary Criticism.

Yemi D. Ogunyemi: (also known as Yemi D. Prince) (Literary Philosopher)

www.ingramcontent.com/pod-product-compliance
Lightning Source LLC
Chambersburg PA
CBHW071721090426
**42738CB00009B/1841**